Your 60 Minute Business Transformation

Save Yourself Blood, Sweat and Tears

Martin Robertson Associates Ltd
5 Kings Court
Falkirk FK1 1PG
Tel: 01324 633550

Your 60 Minute Business Transformation

Save Yourself Blood, Sweat and Tears

Martin Robertson,
Small Business Owner
& Chartered Accountant

Martin Robertson Publishing

This edition published in 2014 in Great Britain by
Martin Robertson Publishing
5 Kings Court
Falkirk
FK1 1PG
www.mraca.com
www.wabt.co.uk

British Library Cataloguing in Publication Data
ISBN: 9780992965600

Typeset in Dante MT Std by Palimpsest Book Production Ltd,
Falkirk, Stirlingshire, Scotland
Printed by Bell & Bain Ltd, Glasgow G46 7UQ

Acknowledgements

Thanks to my family for supporting me; particular thanks to my late sister, Jill, for listening when I needed to be listened to and for believing in me. Jill is a huge loss to family and friends alike.

Thanks to my wife Susanne and daughter Rebecca for inspiring me to live the life I now lead. I love every minute we spend together; the future has never been as exciting!

Thanks to Susanne for formatting and editing the book while coaching me to put it together. I really look forward to us, one day, working to transform people's businesses and lives. I especially look forward to spending more time with you and Rebecca when we are both working four day weeks, forty weeks a year!

Thanks to Seymour Hosking for making me stop to think where I was going with my business ideas. His skilful listening and questioning helped me to take action on the most important ones. Thank you, also, for introducing me to Landmark Worldwide, which has helped me immensely.

Thank you also to Nigel Botterill of Entrepreneurs Circle for planting the seed in my mind about the possibility of writing a book when I attended the Entrepreneurs Circle's Annual Conference in September 2013.

Finally, thanks to Anne and Fiona for their patience and understanding. Their buy-in to my strategy has been key in allowing me to implement the changes that have taken place over the past few years.

Here's some comments made about the book:

"Do you REALLY want your business to succeed? If so, this quick, easy read will definitely set you on your way. I promise that you will feel inspired and better about yourself and your business after reading this . . . there are so many things that resonate and I feel it's given me a nudge in the right direction again, so for me it is definitely worth the money."

David Brice, Paul Bradford Sugarcraft School Ltd

"I really enjoyed your book, it is very true to life and I feel we have experienced similar situations."

Nicola Cattanach, Rooftec (Scotland) Ltd

"I found it to be an easy, enjoyable read which really got me thinking. I would recommend that all business owners read this book. It makes you realise you are not the only one to get a bit stuck, or in a rut, and most importantly that you can get out of it."

Barbara McCallum, Albion Mobility Ltd

"Compelling . . . I couldn't put it down."

Clark Milliken, Clarks Alteration Tailors Ltd

Contents

Foreword

Martin is disarmingly open, honest and forthright about himself and the lessons he's learned in over eighteen years in business. He has created a book that is jam-packed full of precious nuggets of advice and insightful tips.

I particularly love the way that Martin helps small business owners see the importance of the big picture, and makes you realise that big thinking is not just for big corporations – it's for anyone who wants to do, and become, more.

The constant theme throughout this dynamic book is the need for ACTION. By following the advice and recommended actions at the end of each chapter, you cannot fail to make lasting improvements in your business, and major strides towards creating the fulfilling business that you dream of, and deserve.

Richard Lomax, author of *Success in Recession*
Common Sense Marketing

Introduction

This book is my journey. I'm a fairly typical small business owner with over eighteen years of experience in business. It aims to give you, the reader, an opportunity to learn from my many mistakes.

As I know how pressed for time business owners are, I have written this book so that you can read it in around an hour. My recommendation is that you read it through completely, then go back and identify the actions you are going to take to create your dream business.

Each chapter tells you a bit about my story and the pitfalls I encountered, as well as some suggestions for you to consider so that you learn quicker than I did. This book was written with small business owners in mind, new or established; it is a warts and all account and I will share with you some of the mistakes I made – which could have been dealt with earlier had I known how. The suggestions shared should be useful for any business, no matter which line of work you are in. They are not technical, they are not financial, and they are not Profit and Loss or Cash Flow. The suggestions are intended to help you become a better business leader. This book will give you the opportunity to create a fulfilling and inspiring business a lot quicker than I did, no matter which stage you are at.

In my first ten years in business I acted as an employee. For the next three years I was a mediocre manager, then a good manager, before becoming a true leader of my business.

Although in many ways I served a fourteen year apprenticeship I have no regrets; one of my strengths is that I learn from mistakes. . .eventually.

I really know and understand the journey the small business owner makes when they take their first step into self-employment. I understand the optimism at the start. I "get" the worry and fear as we go along. I understand the frustration at the business not turning out the way we wanted it to. More than anything I know the helplessness at not knowing the next step to take.

I also truly understand that in business you have to have special qualities that not all business owners have – the two most important being the ability to embrace change and to be the person who takes ACTION.

My Story

First of all I want to briefly explain my journey to self-employment; so here goes:

I was asked during my very first day as a trainee chartered accountant by the audit manager, "What do you want to do when you qualify?" Without hesitation I answered, "I am going to go into business as a chartered accountant."

When I look back, I ask myself where that answer came from I still had four years ahead of me before I qualified. I can only put it down to my parents' influence. My parents both left secure jobs in the early 1970s to buy a hotel in Burghead, on the Moray Coast, I was only five. It was a time when the fishermen in that area were making a lot of money and quite a few of them enjoyed relaxing in the bar on weekends. I saw first-hand that hard work was financially rewarding.

As time went on, I completely forgot about going into business. I just got my head down and went about qualifying as a chartered accountant, which I did in December 1990. I had wanted to do this since I was 12, and here I was at 25 – qualified but unsure where I was going next. I was lost. I had no vision and I had not thought beyond the point of qualifying.

For a few years I was an auditor, which, for me, was mind-numbingly boring. It amounted to ticking boxes for a living. . .and sometimes counting pigs (I worked in a farming area). I could not get passionate about auditing and it left me totally unfulfilled.

As my thirtieth birthday approached I decided that life was too short for counting pigs, and I handed in my notice (much to the company's delight I think, as by that time my attitude to work was questionable).

The morning after my thirtieth birthday I left for Glasgow, where I slept on a mate's floor for several months, doing various temporary jobs with no idea of what I was going to do for a career. I tried to get various accountancy jobs in industry; however my lack of experience meant that I could not even get an interview never mind a job. It seemed that counting pigs was not a highly valued skill in the city!

Around that time the Glasgow *Herald* newspaper featured a section where self-employed people could advertise their services and businesses. I put an advert in and immediately became the accountant, on a part-time basis, for a land-scaping firm on the south side of Glasgow.

The result of this was that I took the bold decision to open my own accountancy practice on Clarkston Road in February 1996. This decision led to fourteen years of typical self-employment, similar to the hundreds of businesses I now know and have acted for.

Do you sometimes/often/always:

- Work significantly longer hours than you did as an employee? Work evenings and weekends?
- Cancel social engagements because you have work to finish?
- Take fewer holidays than you did as an employee?
- Put in extra hours before holidays so that everything is done before you go?
- Worry for the last few days of your holiday about what you are going back to?
- Find it difficult to relax on holiday, contacting the office to make sure everything is okay?
- Sometimes earn less than you did as an employee?
- Feel continually tired and irritable?
- Wake in the night thinking about the business?
- Feel as if the business controls your life, not the other way around?
- Never find the right staff?
- Follow the crowd, lacking innovation or the guts to be different?
- Feel very good at what you do, e.g. being an accountant, without behaving like the business person you need to be?
- Want to expand the business without really knowing how to?
- Feel lonely, with no one to talk to who understands your position?
- Put suppliers and staff first when it comes to getting paid?

Most small business owners I know identify with some of the above scenarios all too frequently.

By September 2010 I simply accepted that these negative feelings came with being self-employed. To be honest, by then I was worn down – I had lost the passion for my business, and I was left wondering how to change it so that it worked for me. I even considered going to work for someone else. Many business owners I speak to have similar experiences.

In 2010 I took a long holiday. Eighteen days off work was the longest holiday I had taken since becoming self-employed. I decided that I would not think about it while I was away, and I felt the most relaxed I had since I started the business.

On returning home, I decided that I had to do something different if I wanted to have a better future for me and my family. I went along to a seminar where Nigel Botterill of Entrepreneurs Circle talked about the rules of business, one of which was acquiring knowledge. Soon after I picked up a book called *Screw Work Let's Play* by John Williams and that was the start of my self-development journey. The book inspired me to have a think about what it was I enjoyed about being in business. The answer was obvious to me: I loved being in front of clients, listening to them speak about their businesses and being able to make a difference. I knew then what I wanted to happen, though I didn't have a clue how.

Soon after, I attended a Neuro-Linguistic Programming course which helped me learn a great deal. I took a good look at myself and decided that *I* had to change my mindset before the business would change.

I remember listening to the Jim Rohn CD, "The Art of Exceptional Living", where he stated that "self-development comes before business development". This has worked well for me. I started reading personal development books, many of which are listed at the references section at the back of the book. I have signed up to many web newsletters, which have also been useful.

It has taken me three years to get to the point where I can say that I am now truly running a fulfilling and inspiring business. The list above no longer applies to me and I have the confidence to branch into other business areas.

This book is ideal for you whether you:

- are thinking about going into business
- have just started your business
- have been in business for a number of years and are looking for ways to improve it.

It shares with you the mistakes I made from 1996 to 2010; the goal is to help you on your journey – one you may never have dreamt possible.

How to use this book:

If you want to make a return on the time it takes to read this book I have two words of advice: TAKE ACTION.

> "Whatever you can do, or dream you can do, begin it.
> Boldness has genius, power and magic in it."
>
> **Johan Wolfgang von Goethe**

Each chapter has been written with you in mind, I know how difficult it can be to find time to take advantage of any book, especially for a business owner, which is why the whole text should take less than an hour to read.

I recommend:

- Get your notebook out and write down the things that make you think "I must avoid that mistake", or "I am making that mistake". As you do this you will find that you start thinking about alternatives – make sure you write those things down too.
- Highlight the areas of the book most relevant to you.
- Identify areas you would like to work on.
- Identify all the goals you can think of and write them down.
- I like to use mind maps, so if you are happy using them I suggest that you create two mind maps, or two lists or pictures – whichever works for you. Create one for your long term goal and one for the things you are going to work on now. These will take you a step closer to your long term goal.
- I suggest that you find an accountability partner or a mentor or coach, someone you know is successful in your industry or in business in general, and ask them if they would be willing to work with you.

I know how easy it is to create a list of things to do, but I also know how overwhelming they can be when you don't know where to start. I got round this by finding an accountability partner, someone who helped me decide which path to take and where to start.

BE 100% HONEST WITH YOURSELF AND YOUR BUSINESS

TAKE ACTION, NOW!

Visit www.wabt.co.uk to discover how the small business experts can help you create your fulfilling and inspiring business.

"When analysing success people often want to look for 'the one big thing'; the one event or action, the miracle moment that defined breakthrough. The success that these companies built was not based upon one big event, but more a quiet, deliberate process of continuously taking steps in the right direction."

Jim Collins, *From Good to Great*

1

Start With the End in Mind

My Story

In 1996 I left my "cushy" job in a large accountancy practice, with little consideration of the consequences. I decided to start my own accountancy practice, based only on the belief that I was a good accountant. It was to be in the South Side of Glasgow, where I had been living for less than a year. What made this all the more surprising was that when I left the accountancy firm I worked for, I had told myself that I would never work in practice again!

In many ways, I fell into business by default. I hadn't been able to get a job in industry so decided I would start my own accountancy practice.

The first mistake I made, which haunted me until recently, was the fact that I did not have any plan whatsoever for operating and growing a business. At the time I really didn't realise the importance of having a plan, and I didn't know what I *should* have been planning. My main reason for going into business was the necessity to earn a living, like many people. I hadn't stopped to think what services I wanted to provide or who I wanted to sell to, so I just took the opportunities that fell at my feet.

I came from a background of auditing, which did not include an understanding of business or business growth, so consequently I opened my doors with no forward thinking whatsoever. I had never heard of "working on your business" or even much about business planning.

My background also meant that the opportunities that came my way included subcontract audit work for other accountancy practices. I had always disliked auditing – to me it was boring and repetitive and clients did not value the service, but it helped pay the bills, so I did the work without thinking about what that meant for me and my business in the long run.

My second major mistake was that I did not have a picture in my mind of how the business would look when I closed the office door for the last time. I had no targets for:

- The number of clients
- The type of clients
- The unique selling point

- The profits
- The money in the bank
- The number of staff
- The number of offices
- You get my drift!

I dreamed of retiring by forty, yet I hadn't even planned how much money I would need to have by then. I hadn't planned how much I needed the business to be worth. I didn't even have any short term financial projections. Naïve, to say the least!

For some absurd reason I decided to buy brand new office furniture, spending over thirty per cent of all of the money I had. I mean desks, chairs and filing cabinets, it did not include computers! Had I done some planning I would have realised that the money would have been better spent on marketing.

I spent seven years providing auditing, but in the end I hated it so much I stopped providing that service. However this was more to do with the change in legislation around audit requirements than any long term planning on my part.

Although I have never regretted this decision, the consequence of no forward planning meant that once I'd deregistered as an auditor, my fee income fell by thirty percent in two years and I had no growth plan in place to replace it.

It took me a good couple of years to recover financially from this change of direction. Luckily, my wife earned a good salary and was able to support us during the difficult times.

By 2011 I had reached a level of financial security that I was satisfied with because I knew I could pay the bills every month and create a "slush fund" for the business. At that point my focus began to change from making money from accountancy to really wanting to make a difference for my clients and their businesses. I realised that I was running a mediocre business, and I wanted to run a business I loved while creating a way to help my clients do the same. I realised this was my passion and this became my goal, even though I didn't know how I would do it at first.

I tried various different accounting networks and organisations that promised much but didn't provide what I wanted. That was the starting point of my self-development journey. I read lots of business books and attended several self-development training courses. Not everything worked for me, but I never gave up. I always kept the goal of making a difference for clients in mind and although it has taken many years, I have now discovered how I can do that. Reflecting on my experiences in business and my learning of what works has provided me with the knowledge and belief that sharing my journey can reward others both financially and personally.

In the last few years I have never compromised on this goal, I just took a few detours along the way until I found the right path for me.

My Learning

Many of us dream of building our own home. Once you find the plot you get outline plans drawn up, and once they are approved you get the detailed plans drawn. You then think about who you want to build the house and how you are going to fund it. The contractor thinks about who he wants to work with, and so on. Building a business should be no different to building your dream home. No one would start to build a house without planning it beforehand.

Bear in mind:

> "You have to start with a plan, but the plan you start with will not be the plan that gets you there. People make the mistake of thinking they need the perfect plan. There is no perfect plan. By definition, there can't be, because a plan is not getting there – it's only your jumping off point."
>
> **Jeff Olson,** *The Slight Edge*

For every single small business owner, the business always plays a major part in their lives. We have to be clear about what our goals are for the business and what our business is aiming to do. If we don't, then sooner or later, as I found out, the business runs away on its own path and it becomes the boss; it controls our lives – a situation which not one of us had expected when we started out.

I should have considered:

- My services
- My ideal clients
- The difference I wanted to make for clients
- Marketing
- Working on the business
- Employing staff
- Financials.

If you are about to start a business, please, please, start by thinking about it with the end in mind, or at least think where you want to be in ten years time. Think as big as you like but make sure you document your ideas.

Whether you are just about to start in business or you have been in business for fifteen years, goal setting is essential to your success.

In Napoleon Hill's book, *Think and Grow Rich*, he states:

"Man can create anything he can imagine; both poverty and riches are the offspring of thought; and life's battles don't always go to the stronger or faster man, but sooner or later the man who wins is the man who thinks he can."

Big goals are no more difficult than small ones. Remember that you can only achieve what you visualise, which is why I suggest that you have goals for year ten, thinking backwards to year one.

Your aspirations set the ceiling for your success.

I recommend:

- Start your planning for self-employment as soon as you start work. Learn from your boss, and ask yourself:
  - What goes well?
  - What could be done better?
  - What skills can I learn?
- Document your big ideas, use your imagination, and be as wild as you want. Remember your success is only limited by your imagination! Think about the big picture. If you are a visual person create a "Vision Board", if not, write out what your business will be like. Really take time to imagine this. Focus on those things which inspire you to create your ideal business, be it material items such as your dream car or home. If time is your goal, visualise what you will do when taking the entire summer off to be with your kids.
- Think of what you need to have done at the end of year one, in detail, to make sure you are on the right path for the big picture.
- Look at things not as they are, but as they can be.
- If you are preparing a cash flow, be realistic. Once you have prepared your first version double the

costs and half the sales; if you can afford to be in that position then get started.
- Plan for what you really want, not more of the same.
- Ask yourself "if you could have your goal now would you take it?"
- Read books, educate yourself about business, find a free template business plan online to use as your guide. If you search "free business plan template" you'll have many options to guide you. (See Resources section at the end of the book.)
- See www.ted.com for business inspiration.

TAKE ACTION, NOW!

Visit www.wabt.co.uk to discover how the small business experts can help you create your fulfilling and inspiring business.

"A person is a product of their own thoughts. Believe in yourself, believe you can succeed."

David J Schwartz, *The Magic of Thinking Big*

2

Behaviours and Beliefs

Now I want to tell you about some of my beliefs and behaviours which have impacted on my business and held it back.

The first belief I have to mention is more about a lack of belief – specifically, belief in myself. Although I knew I was a really good accountant, with hindsight, I now know that I lacked faith in myself as a businessman and I lacked confidence in what I was providing as a business. As a result, subconsciously, what came across to others was a lack of confidence.

I grew up in a small-town environment, where "blowing your own trumpet" was to be avoided at all costs if you were going to fit in and survive!

This lack of self-belief has had an impact on my business even to this day. After all, if I seemed to lack confidence in my business, why would anyone else have any confidence in it? The legacy of this is most keenly felt in the fees I charge my clients. This has had a direct impact on my profits, my cash flow and ultimately my financial reward from the business.

Examples of this include:

I didn't have a clue about what or how to charge my clients. I didn't know what other accountants were charging for providing the range of services that I did. This lack of knowledge combined with my lack of belief meant there was only going to be one outcome: I charged my clients less than I could or should have, and definitely less than I was worth.

The second belief is the belief that I simply had to make money. This is the case for many of us and it is usually the reason we go into business, so in some respects it's a useful belief to have. In my case I did make some money and my business and I survived those first few difficult years, but I was exhausted and I was certainly not fulfilled. Although I never woke dreading going into work I rarely looked forward to it.

The third belief that has impacted on my business is something that I didn't even realise was holding me back until recently – avoiding confrontation. This has had its uses in keeping me alive (!) but is actually not the healthiest behaviour to display.

Examples of this include:

In eighteen years in business I have very rarely had clients question their fee – after all, I was rarely charging what I was worth. On the handful of occasions they have challenged me I have always backed down and reduced the fee, and every time it irked me because I knew it was because I was avoiding what I perceived to be confrontation. On every occasion I would look at my time records and, the service provided, and think that, what I had charged was reasonable, but rather than have to deal with any unpleasantness, I would give in and reduce their fee.

Not really an empowering behaviour, is it? It usually meant I kept the client but more often than not the person losing out was me.

This also reared its head when it came to the time it took me to issue fees. I would avoid sending out fees until there was little or no money in the bank and I had no choice. By the time the client received the bill they had more than likely forgotten they had even received a service, let alone the value of it! Late feeing would devalue the service for the client and also for me. I would then justify charging less than the service was originally worth to the client so as to avoid confrontation. CRAZY!

Fourthly, I believed I had to be "the saviour" for employees and clients.

Examples of this include:

If an employee came to me and said "Martin, I cannot do 'x'", guess what I would do – I would sort it for them, and probably very quickly. At that moment I thought the best thing was to fix it myself so that the job could be completed.

However, because I could usually do the task really quickly, it suggested to them that they were not as good as me. It made them question their abilities and begin to wonder, "why was it so easy for him?" This kind of "fix it" behaviour can make people feel inadequate and it can drain their self-belief.

Other beliefs and behaviours I could mention here include my fear of rejection and my need to look good – however, I will leave that for another occasion.

My Learning

You will see a theme through the story above was about survival. It's what we are built to do, so I was no different from anyone else. Often when we start, and for those first few years, being in business is about survival. But then what?

Over the years I learnt this:

Life really started to change for me when I began to think seriously about what was important to me about my business. What made me choose to go into business in the first place? What did I really like about the work, and what inspired me to get up every day?

I have now worked out that the most important thing for me is making a difference: helping clients build a business they are proud of, one which fulfils and inspires them. This is important to me and I take the time to work out how I can make a difference. By doing this for clients, my belief in both myself and my business has grown.

I now feel I am making a contribution to my clients' businesses, which makes me very proud and satisfied. What's different for me is that now when I wake up, I know that I am going to be meeting with a business owner who seeks my help to transform their business, and I really look forward to my day.

I have come to know what my services are worth and I charge accordingly.

I know that I have to be flexible with this approach, as the bread and butter of my business is and always will be to provide professional accountancy and taxation services to my clients. I have spent time working on our systems, but I have also delegated much of this work to staff members. I now have more time to spend with my clients discussing their accounts and tax, which often leads to discussing their business needs in broader terms.

We have created a win/win situation out of what were once "staff problems". We have created step-by-step guides that cover most of the professional accountancy and tax matters. When I am confronted with the "I can't do x" problem, I now reply, "Have you checked the guide?" If they are still stuck I will ask them, "If you were me right now what do you think I would do?" I then coach them to decide on the necessary action to perform the task. By not fixing it for them, they learn to do it their way and start to get things right much more often. This means I need to help them less and less.

Another learning point for me has been that the pricing of your product or service is so important. I have since taken the time to work out the going rate for my services, what services I want to provide and for whom. It's often helpful to think about the value you bring to the client – not simply the lowest price. It has also been helpful to fee a client when they can still remember the value of the service they have just received (not six months later).

I am really lucky. I love coming to work every day now. (Is it luck, or is it a result of me taking action to do the things I enjoy?)

Understanding my beliefs and behaviours has been key for me. In the past these may have been useful, comfortable behaviours, but I realised that they were holding me back in certain areas.

In *The Slight Edge* by Jeff Olson, he states "You are on a journey, your life path. That path is a curve, your curve is either upward towards success, or downwards towards failure. The success curve and the failure curve run parallel for a long time. The people living in the success curve take responsibility; live a life that is in some ways uncomfortable, often living outside their comfort zone. The people on the failure curve are comfortable, deceptively comfortable; they are the masses, the nineteen out of twenty. To attain a life that is genuinely comfortable means embracing living uncomfortably for a time."

For me, dealing with my beliefs and behaviours has been uncomfortable, though ultimately I feel as if I am now on the success curve.

I had grown up as a person who displayed BED behaviours that held me back. Characteristics of BED behaviour are:

- Blame
- Excuses
- Denial

I now display OAR behaviour:

- Ownership
- Accountability
- Responsibility

Adopting OAR characteristics has led me from the failure curve onto the success curve.

I recommend:

- Think seriously about what it is that's important to you in your business. What sort of product/service do you want to provide to your customers/clients? What inspires you about this? What would make you want to get out of bed each day?

- When you know what that is, work out the benefit for the client, its value to them, and the appropriate pricing. Do your research and work out what is a reasonable going rate for the level of service you are providing to your customer/client.

- Once you have done the work/provided the service, ALWAYS fee for it as soon as possible. This is when the customer will be at their happiest with the completed work. If you fix their toilet, do you think they value the work you did highest when you sorted it, or three months later?

- Adopt a win/win approach to life and business. This is one of **Stephen R. Covey's 7 habits**. Always go for win/win solutions. To go for win/win, you not only have to be nice, you have to be courageous. You not only have to be considerate and sensitive, you have to be brave.

- Look at how you operate your business; do you have any behaviours which impact negatively on it? Do you need to change?
- I would like to finish by asking. . .are you one of the many business owners who tells themselves "If I don't do it, it won't be done properly?" Or are you one who says "It's my way or the high way?" If you are the latter, make sure you read chapter 5 on systems and what's possible through careful delegation. Things have to be done right, but that doesn't always necessarily mean by you or your way!

TAKE ACTION, NOW!

Visit www.wabt.co.uk to discover how the small business experts can help you create your fulfilling and inspiring business.

"Once you realise that regardless of your business, you really are (and should be) in the marketing business. When you realise this, the business owner moves from thinking of himself as a 'doer of his thing' to being a 'marketer of his thing'."

Glazer-Kennedy Marketing

3

What's Your Business?

My Story

When I started, I didn't have a clue about business, all I knew was how to be an accountant and at that time I did not have any business "know-how". Guess what? I spent almost all of my time being an accountant, rather than properly running a business.

I was proud to tell others that I had my own accountancy practice; however I never described myself as a businessman or, as, an entrepreneur. Looking back I think that was significant.

Primarily, the business grew as a result of being in a great location and from client referrals. As a result of referrals, the business grew at a reasonable pace. I seemingly had no need for any kind of marketing.

In fact, I did very little marketing in the first fourteen years. I can still remember my first set of stationery, featuring purple writing on trendy grey paper. How did I get talked into that? I can only imagine that the printer had ordered it for another job which had been cancelled and he spotted his opportunity to get rid of it to me! Even worse, all the business cards said was the business name and address and that we were Chartered Accountants – we had nothing written on the reverse side of the card, just plain empty space!

One of the referrals led to me working for quite a large and prestigious company and, over time, this generated a large portion of my income. My cash flow and profits were really good and everything in life was great. I bought a fancy new blue BMW and even convinced myself that the impression of success the car gave me would influence potential clients to become clients.

Fantastic, you would think. However, had I opened my eyes and looked at the bigger picture I would have been aware that, firstly, a single employee was becoming very valuable to my business, and secondly, my business was becoming increasingly reliant on one client.

After a few years of everything going smoothly, I began to get the impression that the client wanted to "poach" the employee who had been doing all the work for them. I had a feeling about this but did nothing about it. I naively thought that because I was such a nice guy neither of them would do that to me. WRONG!

Instead of putting a plan in place to encourage the employee to stay with me, or in case both he and the client decided to leave, I took no action. Shortly afterward, the employee left, the client had significantly less need for my services, and my fee income was dramatically reduced overnight.

In a split second I lost my largest and most profitable client and my largest fee earner. A good employment contract and a broader client base would have cushioned the blow, but I had neither.

Now, please do not feel sorry for me, though I certainly felt sorry for myself for a while at the time. It was my own fault; I sensed it was coming yet did nothing to mitigate the consequences. I should have been out there marketing my practice so that the business had a broad client base. I should have had a tighter employment contract for employees and I should have recognised my employee had ambition, and encouraged him to meet those ambitions within my business.

My Learning

All small business owners should stop for a minute and ask themselves, "What is your business?"

Most will say "joiner", "financial advisor", "web designer" etc., just as I did when Nigel Botterill of the Entrepreneurs Circle asked me and I replied that my business was an accountancy practice.

WRONG! My business is the marketing of accountancy, taxation and business transformation services; yours is the marketing of whatever service or product you sell. Can you get to your goal without doing this? Probably not!

Unfortunately for me I was in my fourteenth year in business before I was asked the question.

Always concern yourself with marketing your business – this is a major part of all business owners tasks.

Also, never put all your eggs in one basket. If you have one important client who is generating a significant amount of your profits make sure you use the spare cash to grow your business with other clients, not buy a new car!

Always have a contingency plan for mitigating the loss of valuable employees or clients. Resting on my laurels and not looking further ahead caused me a year or two of grief.

I recommend:

- Understand how to put together a plan for marketing your business.
- Understand the seven most important elements of marketing:
    - Make sure the headline is eye catching.
    - Tell people the benefits of your service or product (scratch their itch!).
    - Use simple positive language, no jargon.
    - Make them an offer they cannot refuse.
    - Give them a freebie – everybody loves a freebie.
    - Create scarcity, only offer the freebie to the first ten to reply to the ad.
    - State the call to action e.g. "Call Martin NOW for your FREE Business Review on 01324 633 550".
- Remember "FAB" when advertising, i.e. "Features and Benefits" – always focus on what features your business has and how this would benefit them.

- Understand the four ways to grow your business:
  - Increase the number of customers you serve.
  - Increase the number of times they come back.
  - Increase the average value of each sale.
  - Increase the systems within your business.
- Get to grips with online marketing (much of it is free):
  - Make sure your website is working for you.
  - Join relevant groups on LinkedIn.
- Learn the art of networking – as people buy from people.

TAKE ACTION, NOW!

Visit www.wabt.co.uk to discover how the small business experts can help you create your fulfilling and inspiring business.

"**Marketing** is the process of communicating the value of a product or service to customers, for the purpose of selling that product or service."

Wikipedia

4

Marketing

My Story

As I said earlier it took me a long time to realise that my business was the marketing of accountancy services and not just being an accountant.

My abiding memory of early marketing is my dull grey business cards with the purple writing; I still cringe when I think about them now.

I remember my first attempts at networking, looking for a friendly face then latching onto them each and every time they were at the same networking events. Even more embarrassing is the memory of our conversations as I tried to sell to them without really knowing them!

I also remember my days in BNI (Business Network International) in Glasgow, where part of the deal was that members had to get up and speak. I have to be honest and say that I was usually awake in the very early hours the night before worrying about my speech. When I got up to speak my throat would be dry, my heart would be pounding and my voice would crack as I struggled to get my words out. For me, speaking in public was the worst thing of all about being in business. I hated it.

I often asked myself, "How am I different from any other accountant?" and as much as I wanted to I could not differentiate my business. I could only come up with the bog standard answers most accountants give, even now:

- I provide a proactive service, contacting clients before their year-end with some tax-saving advice
- I minimise the tax you pay
- I am approachable
- You pay fixed fees
- You pay by monthly standing order.

It drove me mad. I knew that we provided a great service, preparing accounts quickly, being available, and replying to calls, emails, and letters quickly. In fact we are now so confident in our service levels that we state our guarantees on our website. The problem for me has always been that all accountants say the same thing – how I could differentiate from them was constantly on my mind.

Marketing became much more important to me after losing the major client, and after moving to Falkirk in 2005. I did not know anyone in Falkirk who was in business or who needed accountancy services and I would have been lost without my Glasgow-based clients.

I tried various marketing campaigns and employed a range of marketing experts, yet rarely got a good return on my investment. I could not articulate what my unique selling point was to anyone, let alone potential clients.

I cannot possibly comment on marketing without mentioning social media. The biggest mistake I made several years ago was to subcontract my social media, as an early adopter, to a third party. Yet again I had embarked on an important business path and had not set out with the end in mind.

After six months of paying a substantial monthly amount, I pulled the plug. It had not worked for me; we had many followers (which was great), however, the chance of someone living in Portsmouth ever becoming a client of mine, in Falkirk, was remote!

At no point did I ever sit down with the supplier to describe to them what I wanted from this campaign, nor did I tell them about my USP (unique selling point).

Up until I worked out my USP, all the marketing completely and consistently missed the mark. It was all about what I did, not the problems I could solve for clients. I think the growth of my business has been hampered by the fact that only now, in 2014, do I have a USP that I can articulate clearly.

One of the first things I changed when I worked out my USP was my website. I designed my websites with the customer in mind – you can see the results at www.mraca.com and www.wabt.co.uk.

My Learning

My learning has centred on four key things:

- Treat marketing as important to your business as the day to day stuff you do.
- Work out what your unique selling point is in terms of the key benefits you can offer a prospective client.
- Focus all your marketing around these benefits from the point of view of the client.
- Learn to speak about what these benefits are, confidently, to anyone.

I also wanted to share with you some key learning about marketing that made a huge difference for me. Please remember, I am coming from it as the owner of a typical small business, not as a specialist marketer.

I feel that identifying your USP is so important that below I have dedicated a whole section on helping you identify yours:

Questions to help you identify your USP

Make sure your **Unique Selling Point**:

- Tells how you are different
- Aims at your ideal customer
- Grabs attention
- Highlights the benefits of using your service or product.

To help you identify your USP ask yourself:

- How is my service different from my competition?
- What frustrations or fears do my clients have?
- How does my service solve their frustrations or needs?

As a member of the Common Sense Marketing Mastermind Group (run by Richard Lomax) I frequently receive articles featuring marketing advice. Here's one article which stands out for me:

Your Business Success Has Absolutely <u>Nothing</u> To Do With You (It's All About Them. . .Your Customer, Client or Patient)

Everyone else, including your prospects and clients, are <u>also</u> preoccupied with <u>themselves</u>. In fact they are <u>downright indifferent</u> about you.

So Here's Why You Must Change Your Marketing (And your Mind-set)
From GETTING TO GIVING

So. . .

Make sure every advertising or promotional campaign you pay for meets this essential criteria:

- It must create or intensify your prospect's *desire* for the type of product you're selling by presenting the *benefits* it will bring to his or her life.
- It must convince your prospect that the key benefits your product provides *are unique* and therefore unobtainable from any competing product.
- It must leave your prospect feeling that *it is urgent* to at least *enquire about* or *buy* the product as soon as possible.
- It must *compel your prospect to act* – to pick up the phone, visit your website, go to your store and purchase your product at the earliest opportunity.

Then. . .

You must ask yourself does your marketing answer the prospect's questions:

- What's in it for me?
- Will it work for me?
- Why should I believe you?

When speaking to people, when networking or at interviews with potential clients, spend virtually no time talking about what you do or what you know. Instead talk about _the challenges they are facing_ and _the problems they want solving_ and how you can solve them.

Social Media

When it comes to social media, everything above still applies. However you need to be even more specific about what success would look like. Social media can reach anyone in the world at any time. So be clear about the "who" and the "where".

For example it would really have helped me if I had agreed something more specific with my supplier, such as telling them:

"Success, for me, would mean that we have five hundred followers whose businesses operate in the triangle of Perth to Edinburgh to Glasgow, seventy of which have signed up to our newsletter, twenty of which have met with us, and at the end of six months we have ten new clients who we can identify as having come via our social media efforts."

Let me be one hundred per cent clear, all business owners should engage in social media – it cannot be ignored; it is here to stay. I am convinced that social media is going to play a significant part in my businesses growth over the next five years and beyond. Just be very clear about what you want to achieve and be careful how you use it.

I recommend:

- Identify and articulate your unique selling point.
- Have a short statement, no more than three sentences, ready at all times to state simply what you can offer.
- Ask yourself: Who do I want to do business with? Who is my ideal client?.
- Apply the following: "When marketing, remember the real art of making money is in the quality, not the quantity, of the potential clients – hit your target".
- Social media is here to stay. Learn about it, understand the basics and use it to its fullest, no matter your age.
- Personalise your website, and show your character, your USP and your personality through it.
- In all marketing use the following four rules:
    - Tell them how it will <u>benefit</u> them – what problem does it solve?
    - Tell them <u>how</u> it works, and how it's worked for others.
    - Measure your marketing – make sure you know what marketing works for you.
    - Use testimonials to back up your claims.

TAKE ACTION, NOW!

**Visit www.wabt.co.uk to discover how the
small business experts can help you create your
fulfilling and inspiring business.**

To find out more about our USP, see the end of this
book where I tell you what makes Martin Robertson
Associates Ltd different from other accountants.

Note: If speaking in public is your worst nightmare,
that could change if you contact Toastmasters
International like I did.

"A quantum shift is moving from 'doing the work for money' to designing, developing and building a business."

Dan Kennedy, www.gkic.com

5

Working the Business –
Systems and Delegation

My Story

I am embarrassed to admit that when I started in business
I did not think about putting systems in place. It could not
have been further from my mind. When there was only
me to think of, the consequences weren't too drastic.
However, I still had problems and I definitely gave myself
more work than I needed to. Sometimes I did the same
task in different ways, sometimes with different results, and
occasionally with results that I did not want. I made mistakes
and I drove myself mad! I have to admit my stress levels
were high during the early days.

I was not as organised as I would have liked to have been.
It didn't take long for me to realise how inefficient I was
being. Some examples which may make you smile:

- In the early days I did not have a database system for my clients; frequently I would waste fifteen minutes or more looking here and there for a client's details. Worse, I couldn't charge my clients for the time wasted due to my inefficiency. This was a cost to me which could easily have been avoided. It was bonkers!

- The day came when I took on my first employee, who I was planning on training. However, I would often explain to her how to carry out the same sort of assignment in different ways on different days. This would leave her confused and bewildered at times. Then I would get annoyed because she didn't seem to be learning how to do things by herself! Boy, did this highlight the need for systems. The lack of a clear procedure or way of doing things was demoralising and confusing for the employee.

- In the early days I was unable to delegate even the simplest of tasks. Such as:
  - Opening the mail
  - Answering the phone
  - Preparing the letters requesting the clients records
  - Preparing accounts, tax returns and VAT returns
  - Ordering stationery
  - Organising travel.

Many business owners like me work very hard, and yet their businesses don't always work to the same level or give them the reward they desire.

Luckily, I eventually read the great book by Michael E. Gerber *The EMyth*. It had been around for a number of years and I even had it on my bookshelf but I had never read it. When I finally found the time to read it I thought it was brilliant.

Michael E. Gerber will be forever more in my mind for the following quote, "Work on your business, not in your business". I had heard this saying many years ago and even discussed it with clients. The truth is until I read the book I did not know what the saying meant and until three years ago my systems did not work efficiently enough to give me the time to work on my business.

My Learning

There came a point when enough was enough and I decided that I could no longer go on keeping all duties to myself – it was causing me sleepless nights and my employees were becoming disheartened with my inconsistent approach.

I had to learn to delegate and I had to put some systems in place.

What do I mean by systems? Simply, I mean clear and written-down ways of doing things that others (employees) can follow to do the job to the standard that you desire.

Systems – I spent some time and money to:

- identify the jobs I could delegate to others and the jobs I wanted to delegate to others
- defining the best way of doing each of them – a procedure or system
- working out which jobs could use simple IT to make the system more efficient
- have someone to write out the procedure and system.

These "ways of doing things" or systems need not always be complex. They allow anyone to do the job to the standard that you require.

I applied systems to the day-to-day elements of my accountancy practice. I put in systems for preparing accounts, tax returns, vat returns, payroll etc. I continue to review systems regularly to see how they can be improved.

Delegation is not an easy task for most small business owners; most of us are perfectionists and struggle to believe that anyone can do the job to our standard. I finally managed to let go and delegate tasks after years of holding onto them.

What a relief it has been for me to empower my staff to do jobs they are more than capable of doing and to know that they can follow a system or procedure to do the job to the standard I require. We are all much happier as a result.

Benefits I found once I had systemised my business included:

- The business runs more smoothly, more efficiently; it is more organised.
- Jobs are done on time and to budget significantly more often.
- I have taken back control of the business (from it controlling me!).
- My team are more motivated because they see that I trust them.
- My team get more opportunity to develop.
- I know that if the systems are followed the work is carried out to a professional standard.
- The team's level of job satisfaction has improved.
- I get more regular time off, which is very important to me.
- The business works without me being there all the time.
- I have found the time to actually lead the business rather than just manage it and I am now great at delegating, sometimes too good. . .or so my staff tell me.

Richard Lomax of Common Sense Marketing prepared an article entitled "Be the Puppeteer Not The Puppet", some of which I have copied here as it truly captures the difference between working on the business and working in it.

"We all know that to really succeed in business you must work **on** your business, but to be honest most small business owners are too frightened to do it!

"If you fail to work on your business and continue to work in it, all you will ever have is a burdensome and hectic job, laden with all the responsibilities of running a business.

"To be truly worthwhile to your customers and to yourself, your enterprise must become an asset – a machine that delivers glorious service, value and results.

"The only way this is achievable is by you building an enterprise that is led and directed by you, **not** by you rolling up your sleeves and doing the manufacturing, buying, reselling, ordering, cleaning or any puppet activity.

"Once you have put systems in place and can delegate then you have time to build your enterprise. You can take on the role you need to, that is; to be (and continue to be) the visionary, the innovator, the marketing mind, the leader, the director. The puppeteer; not the puppet."

P.S. Did you know that generally a business with great systems is more valuable than one without?

Why is this important?

Because, <u>you</u> are the one person that has the ideas, the vision, and the passion for your product or service. You are the one person who can insist on delivering excellence.

Reading all this again confirms to me that it is only recently that I have become the leader of my business. I am also aware that for many, many years I was not much more than an overworked employee in my own business. At best, I was a manager of others, albeit not a particularly good one.

Every minute you allow yourself to be drawn into daily activities you are doing your customers and yourself a disservice, and you are taking your eye off the business.

The big mistake I made was to stop at accounting and office systems; I didn't apply it anywhere else in the business. My big learning point was that I really should have put a system in place for all areas, especially marketing.

Michael E. Gerber also, states, "The real key to your influence with me is your example, your actual conduct." Guess who put the systems in place but didn't always follow them, because of a lack of time? Me, and it only led to staff taking the same short cuts as I took. I know now that if there is a system in place it has to apply to all, otherwise sooner or later shortcuts will be taken leading to mistakes.

I have to lead properly. . .by example!

I recommend:

- "Start with the end in mind" – Establish exactly how you want the business to be, in your own mind, before thinking about systems, particularly the quality and standard of the work to be done. Once you are clear about these things document your thoughts.
- Create a document detailing what you want to achieve through systemisation.
- Put systems in place as early as possible.
- Systemise all areas of your business including:
    - Dealing with suppliers
    - Operations
    - HR
    - Marketing
    - Sales
    - Accounting records.
- Use IT if it helps with efficiency.
- Review and update systems regularly; if they are not working, change them.
- Involve staff in designing them.
- Measure the systems to manage them.

TAKE ACTION, NOW!

Visit www.wabt.co.uk to discover how the small business experts can help you create your fulfilling and inspiring business.

"Communication is the most important skill in life."

Stephen R. Covey,
The Seven Habits of Highly Effective People

6

Communication

My Story

When I was twelve I had an eye accident and lost the sight in my right eye. It was a very traumatic event for me. As I look back I have realised that the accident not only had a huge impact on my sight, but also on my ability to communicate.

For seven years afterwards I was too embarrassed to make eye contact with anyone I didn't know, and with many that I did. This was during my formative teenage years and early adulthood. It made connecting with new people and talking to them properly very difficult.

If I'm being honest, communication was never my strongest skill. It amazes me when I look back how I managed to survive in business in the early years.

In business you communicate on a daily basis with, amongst others:

- your customers
- potential customers
- your staff
- your suppliers
- your family when you go home stressed after a hard day's work.

Here are some examples of my communications which still make me cringe:

When accounts are in draft form I review them and the files supporting the figures. Before, I would review them in my office. I would usually have the door open and the employee would be in the next room, within earshot. I would be getting frustrated while reviewing the accounts and saying things under my breath like, "I can't believe this is the same mistake again," etc. You get the drift. It became such a bad habit for me that sometimes the words would be out of my mouth before I realised and the employee would hear me. The poor employee would be fretting about what was upsetting me, and slowly losing their confidence in their ability to do their job. This communication was toxic for both me and the employee.

I always now review the draft accounts in front of the person who prepares them. This has been very successful as they know what is expected of them. The results have been fewer mistakes.

Another example was when an employee asked me for help. Often I would still be thinking about what it was that I had been doing and just wanted to get back to that as quickly as possible (because I thought that what I was doing was more important). I was not really listening to the problem being presented. Nor was I reading the situation to get to the heart of the matter or checking that the employee had understood what I had asked them to do. My communication would often be confusing. Later, when I reviewed the work they had done I couldn't understand why it wasn't done properly. I would be annoyed and often the employee and I would disagree on what had been said. My coaching skills were non-existent then. I have improved my listening and communication skill: there is less confusion now.

Some of my worst communications were with myself! All of us have a voice in our head (no, I'm not crazy). It's the voice that reminds us of what we need to do and often asks, "What will people think of me?" If there was a way to interpret an event or conversation in a negative way I could guarantee you I would. The classic example was whenever a letter came into the office in a brown envelope. I would know it was from HM Revenue & Customs and would immediately panic, before I had even opened the envelope! I expected it to be bad news for a client and the voice in my head would go to work.

If I met a potential client and they said they would contact me and didn't, the voice in my head would be saying it was because they probably did not like me or I had done or said something wrong. In reality, they may just have been too busy to contact me or they may have decided they didn't want the hassle of changing accountant. There could have been a hundred reasons. How could I know what was going on in their lives?

Over the years I have learnt how to control my fears and unhelpful thoughts; it is much more than just thinking positively. Only recently I read the fantastic book *The Chimp Paradox* by Dr Steve Peters, which I cannot recommend highly enough if you want to gain a better understanding of how to get your brain under control.

These are small examples and there are many more which created a stressful life. But there were also the thoughts that had a bigger impact on my business. I told myself that I did not want a big business. One of the biggest reasons that my business remained small was the voice in my head telling me to take the safe option every time.

My Learning

My biggest learning point has been that, on the assumption that there is a market for my service, my success will depend entirely on how I communicate. This will be the same for any business. My success over the next twenty years will depend on the quality of the internal thoughts I have and how I translate them into actions.

To be successful you need to communicate with conviction about the benefits and value of what you do and how well you do it. To do it well you need to look people in the eye and believe in yourself.

Have you gone through years of employing staff with varying degrees of success? Have you gone home many a night and complained about the staff? I used to, however, that changed when I went to an NLP Business diploma course. The first question I was asked was, "Why are you here?" Automatically I replied, "I am always having problems with staff, they make too many mistakes, they are too slow. Yet the only constant in this over the past fourteen years is me. I must be doing something wrong."

That was a big light bulb moment for me and I realised that each of us interprets what is going on around us in many different ways. As a result, it's important to check that I have understood what has been said to me and that what I have said has been understood in all my communications. Clarification is vital.

I also realised that even when I thought I was listening, I was really listening in readiness to reply rather than to understand fully what was being said. In conversations I was either speaking or preparing to speak and not really listening to what was being said and, just as importantly, to the way it was being said.

Stephen R. Covey's book *The 7 habits of highly effective people* goes into a lot of detail about listening, and the most important learning for me was to "seek first to understand then to be understood".

Dealing with the voice in my head has been a tougher challenge. On a recent personal development course I learned that the voice is in all of us and will never go away. It helps us to survive, to fit in and to manage our daily existence – however, the trick is to deal with the facts. Make sure you clarify understanding whenever you can. It can take courage to seek out the facts, but once you do, you can be clearer and life and work become much less stressful!

I recommend:

- If a communication goes wrong, stop and think about it from the other person's point of view. Ask yourself – what would I do differently next time?
- When instructing your employees to carry out a task make sure that your instructions are clear and precise, (eg. what, when, where, how) and that they understand what is expected of them – even get them to repeat it back to you.
- Learn to listen properly. Don't just wait to speak.
- Be aware of the voice in your head. When it "speaks" unhelpful negative thoughts ask yourself, "What are the facts here? What is it that I really know to be true?"
- Read Stephen R. Covey's book *The Seven Habits of Highly Successful People*.
- Seek ways to improve all of your communications, whether it is through reading books or attending courses. The results impact your whole life for the better, not just your business life.

TAKE ACTION, NOW!

Visit www.wabt.co.uk to discover how the small business experts can help you create your fulfilling and inspiring business.

Conclusions – What Next?

When I started writing this book, my main hopes were that reading about my mistakes and the things I have learned would be useful for other small business owners, and that it would help them avoid making the same mistakes I did, or at least that it would provide a bit of advice for moving forward.

As I've been writing it I've realised that advice is great, however, anyone can read and listen to all the advice in the world, but the only thing that will make a difference to you, your business and your life is if **YOU TAKE ACTION**.

At the beginning, I advised that you make a note of what strikes you as useful in the book, where you have had similar experiences, what you need to change and what actions you could take. Now I ask you to reflect on those notes. Review where you recognise yourself and your business, and consider which action would be useful. But BEFORE you write yourself a "to do list", ask yourself:

What's stopped me from doing anything about this before?

Be 100 per cent honest with yourself. There could be many reasons and all are valid. But, however valid the reasons, the outcome, your life, your business, will remain the same unless YOU do something different.

As Henry Ford, Founder of the Ford Motor Company put it. . .

"If you always do what you've always done you always get what you've always got."

All the issues and problems you have in your business will remain, whatever the reasons, unless you **DECIDE** to make a change, **TAKE ACTION**, and keep on taking action.

"It's important for you to get clear for yourself that your only access to impacting life is action. The world does not care what you intend, how committed you are, how you feel or what you think and certainly has no interest in what you want and don't want. Take a look at life as it is lived and see for yourself that the world only moves for you when you act."

Werner Erhard, Founder, EST

So my challenge to you is to **TAKE ACTION**. It actually doesn't matter that much where you start, just start and then keep on going. Create a new habit, a habit that will make a positive difference to you, your life and your business.

A small step every day will, in time, take you on a journey. Just make sure it's the direction you want to be going in.

"Be not afraid of going slowly; be afraid only of standing still."

Chinese Proverb

Finally

"Many small business owners have an aggravated case of business astigmatism (blurred or distorted vision) which could be cured if they would do the obvious thing of calling in some business specialist to correct their vision and give them a true view of their own business and methods."

This quote was taken from a book entitled *Obvious Adams* by R. R. Updegraff. It's a book that was written in 1916. Nearly a century later, this quote is still highly relevant. Up until 2010, I was one of those small business owners suffering from "business astigmatism". I didn't have anyone to call on for help, I didn't have anyone to bounce ideas off and I didn't have anyone to challenge my thinking. For years I had to work out things for myself.

Through my learning, I have now transformed my business and I am now transforming others: I can work with you to help you do the same. I can help you see your business more clearly and create a vision that's important to you, AND I can help you to take the action you need to.

My goal is to work with a select few business owners who want to leave mediocrity behind and live a business life they love.

My business mission is to make a positive and long lasting difference to clients' businesses and lives, so that they make more money, have more time to enjoy it and build a business that fulfils and inspires them. In the process, I hope that this approach creates long lasting sustainable businesses that create jobs.

"Good companies became great by becoming brutally honest, having strong and dedicated leaders and workers and also by finding answers to these three questions:
1. What can we be the best in the world at?
2. What drives our economic engine?
3. What are we deeply passionate about?"

Jim Collins, *From Good to Great*.

Do you want to see your business more clearly? Do have the courage to be challenged, to TAKE ACTION and to be held accountable for your business success? If so pick up the phone, dial 01324 460 288 and ask for Martin, I WILL HELP YOU. I will get you to do the things you have been avoiding that will get you the business you have always wanted.

An offer from Martin Robertson for readers of *Your 60 Minute Business Transformation*

Dear Reader

Thank you for reading my book. I'm honoured that you took the time to read this far! Assuming that you have found it to be value for money and that it has inspired you to take action, the great news for you is there are more ways that I can help you.

You can connect with me through www.wabt.co.uk where you can sign up for regular business inspiration, newsletters and a **FREE** monthly webinar where time is spent helping you deal with **your** business issues. You can send me your question or issue in advance and I will help you deal with whatever it may be.

At Business Transformers we have created tailored work-shops aligned to the ideas in this book, which will help anyone from small business new starts, to the budding tycoon, through to those who have been in business for many years and need to be re-energised, who want to be super successful.

In addition, we can work with you, one to one, at times convenient to you, to hold you accountable for your dreams and aspirations and to give you the best chance of actually doing the things you know you need to do.

We, also, are putting together a schedule of monthly busi-ness transformation mastermind groups. Find out more from our website www.wabt.co.uk

Also, if you are thinking of going into business we offer a unique service which will give your business the best possible chance of success or even help you avoid business failure, saving you a lot of heartache and disappointment in the long term. You never know, we may even help you identify another business opportunity in the process!

How do we do this?

- We work with clients to identify what they really want from their business and what's important to them.
- We help them create a vision for their business future.

- We help them identify actions to move them towards their goal in a strategic way.
- We help them work through these actions and deal with things that might be stopping them.
- We share our commercial awareness to support business success.
- We hold YOU accountable so that you do take ACTION!.
- We create a brief monthly business transformation plan measuring the important numbers in the business.

Since September 2010 I have invested over £120,000 in time, training and buying resources, and continue to invest thousands per month to make sure that we are true business experts.

Phone me NOW, on 01324 460 288, to discuss how you can take advantage of this investment and how I can help transform your business and your life.

P.S.Note: Just in case you need any more convincing, it is appropriate to let you know that all of my Business Transformation services come with a 100% money back guarantee. You did read that right, **I give a 100% guarantee with all Business Transformation services provided**.

P.P.S. BE QUICK or join the waiting list!

Testimonials

"Since I started my transformation sessions my turnover, profitability, work life balance, happiness and enjoyment have all increased hugely, and that's no co-incidence."

David Brice of Paul Bradford Sugarcraft School Ltd

"Martin's passion and enthusiasm for guiding and helping others has got us excited and given us back that sense of excitement and buzz. I would highly recommend business transformation for other business owners."

Carol Anderson of June Brides Ltd

"Every meeting we have helps us to regain control of our business. We are improving our business every day, learning new skills, growing as people, re-energized and are now optimistic about our business future. If you are fortunate enough to employ them we are certain you will be as delighted as we are."

Barbara McCallum, Albion Mobility Ltd

"It was a very positive experience which helped me move forward with my business in ways I wouldn't have achieved on my own."

Craig Holland, Vivid Walls

"The changes since we started working with you have been phenomenal."

Mark Cattanach, Rooftec (Scotland) Ltd

"Being a small business owner can be a lonely road, with potholes at times, and wide open roads others. Business transformation sessions have helped me see the road ahead clearly and re-kindle my passion for my business."

Clark Milliken, Clarks The Alteration Tailor Ltd

Would you like to run a business that truly fulfils and inspires you? Then the first thing you have to do is TAKE ACTION, NOW!

Contact me NOW on 01324 460 288 or visit our website at www.wabt.co.uk.

Book References

Collins, J. (2001) *From Good to Great, Why some companies make the leap. . .and others don't.* Random House, London.

Covey, S. R., (1989), *The 7 Habits of High Effective People: Powerful Lessons in Personal Change.* Simon and Schuster UK Ltd, London.

Gerber, M. E., (1995) *The E Myth Revisited: Why most businesses don't work and what to do about it.* HarperCollins, New York.

Hill, N., (1937), *Think and Grow Rich.* Embassy Book Distributors, Mumbai.

Olson, J. (2005), *The Slight Edge*, publisher (?)

Rohn, J. (1994) *The Art of Exceptional Living*, Audio CD, Simon and Schuster UK Ltd, New York.

Schwartz, D. J. (1995), *The Magic of Thinking Big: Set your goals high. . .then exceed them.* Simon and Schuster UK Ltd, London.

Sugars, B. J. (2006), *Instant Systems.* McGraw Hill, New York.

Williams, J., (2010), *Screw Work Let's Play: How to do what you love and get paid for it.* Pearson Education Ltd, Harlow.

Updegraff, R. R. (1926) *Obvious Adams; the story of a successful businessman.* Firepole Marketing, US.

Internet Resources

General Business inspiration

http://www.ted.com

Guide to free business plan templates

http://blog.thecompanywarehouse.co.uk/2012/06/18/4-free-business-plan-templates-where-to-find-them-and-what-you-get/

http:bgateway.com/starting-up/business-plan-template/

GKIC

http://gkic.com/

Lomax, R. (2013) Be the Puppeteer Not the Puppet.

http://www.common-sense-marketing.com/blog/be-the-puppeteer-not-the-puppet/

Marketing Advice

http://www.common-sense-marketing.com
http://www.nigelbotterill.com

Public speaking

Toastmasters International

http://www.toastmasters.org/

Personal development

Landmark Worldwide

http://www.landmarkworldwide.com

Actions I Am Going To Take

_____

_____

_____

_____

_____

_____

_____

_____

_____

_____

_____

_____

_____

_____

_____

_____

_____